CATHOLIC UPDATE GUIDE TO VOCATIONS

D1540305

Catholic Update
guide to
Vocations

MARY CAROL KENDZIA,
Series Editor

Franciscan
MEDIA
Cincinnati, Ohio

Nihil Obstat: Hilarion Kistner, O.F.M.
Imprimi Potest: Fred Link, O.F.M.
RESCRIPT
In accord with the *Code of Canon Law*, I hereby grant my *Imprimatur*
the *Catholic Update Guide to Vocations.*
Most Reverend Joseph R. Binzer
Vicar General and Auxiliary Bishop
of the Archdiocese of Cincinnati
Cincinnati, Ohio
April 17, 2012

The *Imprimatur* ("Permission to Publish") is a declaration that a book or pamphlet is considered to be free from doctrinal or moral error. It is not implied that those who have granted the *Imprimatur* agree with the contents, opinions or statements expressed.

Scripture passages have been taken from *New Revised Standard Version Bible*, copyright ©1989 by the Division of Christian Education of the National Council of the Churches of Christ in the U.S.A., and used by permission. All rights reserved.
Excerpts from the documents of Vatican II are adapted from the versions available at www.vatican.va.

Cover and book design by Mark Sullivan
Cover image © PhotoXpress | Luuk81

LIBRARY OF CONGRESS CATALOGING-IN-PUBLICATION DATA
Catholic update guide to vocations / Mary Carol Kendzia, series editor.
p. cm.
Includes bibliographical references.
ISBN 978-1-61636-432-8 (alk. paper)
1. Christian life—Catholic Church. 2. Vocation—Catholic Church. 3. Catholic Church—Doctrines. I. Kendzia, Mary Carol.
BX2350.3.C383 2012
248.4'82—dc23
2012011464
ISBN 978-1-61636-432-8

Published by Franciscan Media
28 W. Liberty St.
Cincinnati, OH 45202
www.FranciscanMedia.org

Printed in the United States of America.
Printed on acid-free paper.
12 13 14 15 16   5 4 3 2 1

Contents

About This Series

The Catholic Update guides take the best material from our best-selling newsletters and videos to bring you up-to-the-minute resources for your faith. Topically arranged for these books, the words you'll find in these pages are the same clear, concise, authoritative information you've come to expect from the nation's most trusted faith formation series. Plus, we've designed this series with a practical focus—giving the "what," "why," and "how to" for the people in the pews.

The series takes the topics most relevant to parish life—e.g., the Mass, sacraments, Scripture, the liturgical year—and draws them out in a fresh and straightforward way. The books can be read by individuals or used in a study group. They are an invaluable resource for sacramental preparation, RCIA participants, faith formation, and liturgical ministry training, and are a great tool for everyday Catholics who want to brush up on the basics.

The content for the series comes from noted authors such as Thomas Richstatter, O.F.M., Lawrence Mick, Leonard Foley, O.F.M., Carol Luebering, William H. Shannon, and others. Their theology and approach is grounded in Catholic practice and tradition, while mindful of current Church practice and teaching. We blend each author's style and approach into a voice that is clear, unified, and eminently readable.

Enrich your knowledge and practice of the Catholic faith with the helpful topics in the Catholic Update Guide series.

Mary Carol Kendzia
Series Editor

Introduction

There has long been a tendency in the Church to apply the term *vocation* only to Holy Orders and religious life. Yet St. Paul himself gives us a broader notion of vocation or calling. He said that all have been called to fellowship with Jesus (see 1 Corinthians 1:9), and insisted that Jesus died for all (see 2 Corinthians 5:15). We can say, then, that all people have a vocation, a calling from God, to share in the redemption and eternal life Jesus came to bring. It is significant that when the bishops at the Second Vatican Council wrote about the Church, they repeated Paul's conviction, "All humanity is called to belong to the new People of God" (*Lumen Gentium*, 13).

The Greek word for "Church" is *ekklesia*, which means literally "those who have been called." The official call to membership in the Church comes through our baptism. Canon law refers to the baptized as "the Christian faithful" and emphasizes that all the faithful have an obligation to spread the Gospel.

Some of the baptized are known as the laity, that is, "the people." Some are called to hierarchical office (to Holy Orders) to serve the people, and they are known as deacons, priests, or bishops. Some are called to religious life, that is, a vowed life of poverty, chastity, and obedience. Some are called to married life, and others to single life. All, however, are called to faithfulness and to holiness.

A reporter once asked Pope John XXIII what he considered the most important day in his life. The newsman expected the Holy Father to say, "The day I was named bishop of Rome," or "The day I decided to call an ecumenical council." Instead the vicar of St. Peter said, "The day I was baptized." Blessed Pope John XXIII knew that baptism is the first and most important call in a Christian's life; the subsequent calls (single life, marriage, priesthood, or religious life) are interpreted and lived in the light of that initial vocation.

The *Catholic Update Guide to Vocations* is a review of the four vocations or states of life in which the Christian faithful live the Gospel. The laity, whether married or single, are especially responsible for bringing the Gospel into the secular world. The Christian faithful who marry are bound to build up the people of God through the witness of their marriage and the promotion of family life. Clerics have the obligations of pastoral ministry in the Church. Those in consecrated life have the duty to seek perfection by vows of poverty, chastity, and obedience, giving witness through lives of charity to others and of praise to God.

CHAPTER ONE

Primary Vocation, Secondary Vocations

Your Primary Vocation

A Christian's first calling is to belong to the people of God—to accept Jesus as Lord, to become a disciple, and to participate in his plan of salvation by giving witness and spreading the Gospel. The Christian's second vocation is the way he or she lives out the primary one.

The *United States Catholic Catechism for Adults* addresses this issue, explaining that Jesus does not think of the people of God as a nameless people in a faceless crowd. Rather, Jesus calls each of us by name, and each of us has a vocation—whether we are clergy, religious, laypeople, married, single, adults, or children. The *Catechism* teaches that each person has a unique role to play in the divine plan for salvation.

Sr. Fidelis Tracy, C.D.P., develops this recognition of our primary and secondary vocations. She explains that to be created is to be called by God, and the mystery of vocation is part of God's love for us. Sr. Fidelis remembered learning as a small child in religion class that God loves us and keeps creating us day by day. Everyone, in fact, is continually being called by God, and each of us sooner or later asks if we are following our call to holiness. She says that, at the core of each person is a primary vocation. It is a call to holiness, to becoming a living response to God's love. This call is common to everyone, but responding to God's love is going to be unique and particular for each person. The first two steps in discovering how we are to live out our vocation to holiness are simple but complex. We must know ourselves, and be honest about our dreams and capabilities. This personal assessment gives us clues about what kind of secondary vocation may be ours.

Discovering God's calling is not like solving a mystery laid out for us in a novel or TV show. God will not trick us into a particular way of life. Rather, God is gracious.

There are a number of paths toward the goal of union with God. Our call will be manifest when we become like Jesus: compassionate, forgiving, loving, and healing toward others. If we think about people in our lives whom we would readily call holy, we would think of neighbors who reached out to those in need. Or we might associate holiness with courage in adversity,

2

a courage that comes from faith. Holiness is manifested in selfless love, forgiveness, and service.

Service or ministry is not for a chosen few. It is mandated by our baptism. We can serve in such Church-related ministries as religious education, pastoral care of the sick, serving meals in a soup kitchen, and caring for children or aging parents. As baptized Christians we participate in the life and mission of Jesus by attending to the needs of others. One does not need to be a priest or religious in order to work in a parish, school, hospital, social service organization, or as a missionary among the poor. All these ministries can be done by people who are neither clerics nor vowed religious.

Discerning Your Secondary Vocation

Fr. Mark Thibodeaux offers some insights into the process of discerning our secondary vocation. Should we stay single, get married, be ordained, or take the vows of religious life? He explains that we Christians don't just decide things, we *discern* them. That is, we do our best to figure out what God is calling us to in every situation. We do our best to say yes to that divine invitation. But *how* do we discern God's will for us?

There are a number of approaches to discernment in the Catholic tradition. One of the best comes from St. Ignatius of Loyola, founder of the Jesuits, who lived in Europe during the sixteenth century. His insight was this: "Good discernment consists of prayerfully pondering the great desires that well up in my daydreams."

Many spiritual writers of Ignatius's day spoke of desire as an obstacle to God's will. One solution was to suppress one's desires—to eliminate them whenever possible. Ignatius, on the other hand, held the radical notion that God dwells in the desires of a good person. Not only are desires not evil, but they are one of God's primary instruments of communicating his will to his children.

Ignatius believed that God enflames the heart with holy desires, and with attraction toward a life of greater divine praise and service. He did not seek to quash desires, but rather sought to tap into the deepest desires of the heart, trusting that it is God who has placed them there.

Desires, of course, play a role in our sinful choices, too. But Ignatius would define sin as *disordered* desire. The problem is not that we *have* desires, but that they are *disordered* within is. That is why we must begin this entire process by tapping into the greatest, most universal desire among humans: to praise, reverence, and serve God. We fall into sin when we are ignorant of the motives beneath the desires. Consider this way of understanding personal sin: We sin, not because we are in touch with our desires but precisely because we are *not* in touch with them! This is one of Ignatius's most profound insights.

How, then, do we tap into these great desires? We daydream, that's how! We fantasize about great and beautiful futures. We let God dream in us and we sit in silent awe and wonder as these holy dreams come to life before the eyes and ears of our souls. Now that's a different approach to prayer than most of us know. But that's what St. Ignatius taught.

If we have to choose among several different options, we might start with one option, and ask God to show us the marvelous things he could do with this possibility. We can think crazy thoughts and mull over preposterous proposals. We can have galactic visions of new worlds of possibilities opening up merely by saying yes to God's invitation to that option. Then we start all over again and dream about a second option, a third one, and so on.

We might begin by asking ourselves the big question: "What is my purpose in life?" Of course, the answer Catholics learned as children applies: "to praise, reverence, and serve God." Now, we begin to daydream—or better—to *pray-dream!* To prayerfully explore our options, we must pray-dream all the possibilities.

As we pray-dream the possibilities of living out our great desires in each option, we can try to note the stirrings in our hearts, and ask ourselves:

- Which of these dreams leave me filled with holy and whole-some desires?

- Which leave me with a sense of closeness to God?
- Which leave me filled with faith? With hope? With love?
- Which make me want to go out and share them with the people I love?
- Which leave me with a deep-down peace and tranquility? With a sense of rightness?

Then we discern which dreams leave us in desolation. We ask ourselves:

- Which leave me without faith? Without hope? Without love?
- Which leave me with a sense of distance from God?
- Which leave me disquieted and agitated?
- Which leave me with no passion and zeal? With a sense of boredom and tepidity?
- Which fill me with deep-down anxiety and fear?
- Which are the dreams I'm not very excited to talk about with my mentors or friends?

As we dream these pray-dreams, we pay particular attention to the fluctuating moments of peace vs. disquiet, and of impassioned energy vs. deflatedness.

Ignatius says that when a well-intentioned, prayerful person is in sync with God, God's will comes "sweetly, lightly, gently, as a drop of water that enters a sponge." This inner peace—even for a tough decision—is one of the most important signs of

God's will. Often, after many hours of prayerful deliberation, there will be a moment when you just know. It will feel not as though you are *making* a decision but, rather, as though you are *acknowledging* a decision that has already been agreed upon by God and your heart.

Deciding is not an easy task. Discerning God's will is even more challenging! But Ignatius assures us that God has placed his desire deep within the desires of our own hearts. Pray-dreaming allows us to ponder those deep desires, and to discover and say yes to God's grace-filled path for each of us.

Reviewing the Options

The next four chapters of this *Catholic Update Guide to Vocations* are devoted to the four possibilities for a Christian's secondary vocation. Our primary vocation, you will remember, is to accept Jesus as Lord, to live according to the Gospel, to spread the Good News by word and deed. Spiritual writers often describe it as "the call to holiness." Through baptism we become official members of the Church. We become "the faithful."

The secondary vocation is the state in life in which the faithful respond to the primary call. The four secondary vocations are single life, marriage, Holy Orders, and religious life. The faithful include the laity, clerics, and those in religious life. Those in Holy Orders (deacons, priests, bishops) are called "clerics"; those in religious life (monks, nuns) are known as "religious." All the others make up "the laity," or "laypeople."

Discernment of one secondary vocation does not necessarily rule out another secondary vocation. Most priests of the Roman Catholic Church are not married, but some are. Deacons are men who have received the first order of Holy Orders (they are clerics, not laymen) but many are also married. By definition the single and the religious are not married, but some religious may have also received Holy Orders.

Questions for Reflection

1. What is the primary vocation of every Christian?
2. How do the single people you know feel about their state in life? Are some just waiting for the right person to come along for marriage? Is being single a conscious choice for others?
3. Have you ever "pray-dreamed?" What was it like?

CHAPTER TWO

The Single Life

In her book *Party of One: Living Single With Faith, Purpose, and Passion*, Beth M. Knobbe challenges several myths about the single life and proposes that single life can rightly be called a vocation. Although she speaks directly to those who have never been married, she offers encouragement to the widowed, divorced, and separated as well.

She explains that we live in a couples' world. But it is not God's plan for everyone to marry or for everyone to have children. We can each be a complete person on our own. Through her own reflections, she realized that it's OK to have your own identity, your own friends, your own personal thoughts and feelings. The key to a fulfilling single life is to believe that you can be a complete person on your own.

* * *

While growing up, I heard a lot about vocations, always presented as a call to married life, religious life, or single life. The single life, however, was never given much credence, and the idea of choosing to be single was usually presented as a last resort.

Discovering one's vocation is more than deciding whether to get married, join the seminary, or enter a religious community. Finding your vocation in life answers the questions, "Who will be your friends?" and, "How do you want to be with them?" I want to be with people in such a way that I can share my passion for God and live a life of service to others. This is something I have known for a very long time. It is my true calling in life; it is who I am. The more I reflected on this, the more I realized that the best way to live out this call is as a committed single person.

My choice to be single for the moment is not a choice to avoid relationships. In some ways, I'm actually choosing to be in deeper relationships with others. As single people, we often look for love and affection from people of the opposite sex. When I stopped looking for dating relationships, I developed closer relationships with my girlfriends, and I was free to enter into greater friendships with my guy friends. I had a wonderful and ever deepening relationship with God through prayer and found greater fulfillment through involvement with my church.

Not everyone is called to a life of intentional singleness. I suspect many who find themselves single wish their circumstances were different. Singles sometimes struggle with loneliness, anxiety, fear, pressure from family, and self-worth. Likewise, we are inclined to believe that the grass is greener on the other side of the relationship fence. Singles may think that married people have it all together, or that married couples miss the carefree spirit of their single years. Marriage isn't easy; single life isn't easy either.

Myths About Single Life

#1 *Life Begins at Marriage*—Many of us grew up with an image of a happily-ever-after ending. Many singles live with the myth that we need to wait until we are in a relationship before we can live the kind of life we want. Life does not start the moment you walk down the aisle. Life is happening in front of your very eyes! It is not a dress rehearsal for when you have a relationship.

#2 *Marriage Equals Wholeness*—Many people view marriage as a requirement to attain happiness. Being an integrated, whole person is not dependent on being connected to someone else. If you are not happy on your own, chances are it is going to take more than a relationship to resolve your discontent.

#3 *You Are Not an Adult Until You Are Married*—For some people, marriage is the ultimate mark of adulthood. They think it is proof that you have arrived in the world of grown-ups. In fact, adulthood can be defined by age, but it is also characterized by the moments that catapult us into maturity. It can be discouraging when we recognize that single people are subjected to different expectations from married people. This happens when singles are passed over for promotions and when people make assumptions about our financial priorities. It takes a certain amount of wisdom to reflect on our single years and say, "I'm OK with the place where I am right now."

#4 *Singles Want to Be Set Up*—Although they mean well, it can be incredibly awkward when friends want to set us up with a date. Even worse is the pressure from family members to find a mate, make your way down the aisle, and provide grandchildren before it is too late. Sometimes I want to scream, "My life isn't broken!" Being single isn't a problem that needs to be "solved" or an issue that needs to be "fixed."

#5 *All Singles Should Consider Religious Life*—For the record, I have considered joining a religious community. While I haven't ruled it out completely, I'm pretty sure it's *not* where God wants me. The single life is a great time to learn and practice the tools of discernment. Ultimately we can trust that our future is in God's hands, and God is leading us toward that next step, whatever it may be.

#6 *Being Single Means Being Alone*—I have learned there is a big difference between being alone and being lonely. Married people experience loneliness. In the spiritual life the word *soli-*

tude best expresses the contentment we feel when we are at peace with our aloneness. Spiritual writer Henri Nouwen reminded us that solitude is where we find our identity, the place where we are with God and God alone. In the busyness of life, most people find that a bit of downtime goes a long way to provide respite for our weary bodies. Solitude is not only possible but necessary for us to thrive in the single life.

#7 *Men and Women Can't Just Be Friends*—When it comes to our acquaintances with people of the opposite sex, inquiring minds always want to know if there is something more to our friendship. Perhaps this stems from a cultural expectation to be married. I'd like to suggest that men and women can indeed be friends, without the added pressure of something more. There is value in getting to know a person even without physical attraction. Friendships are essential to the single life. They are a source of intimacy, connection, laughter, and fun.

#8 *The Church Cares Only About Couples and Families*—Early in my young adult years, I was blessed to find a faith community filled with married and single people of all ages and stages of life. I made great friends, we supported one another in our faith, and together we discerned the choices to which God had called each of us. Unfortunately, my experience is not shared by all single people. There is a wonderful phrase that has been used to describe the challenge of working in multicultural congregations which says, "the house of God is holy not just because all are welcome there, but because all belong there." I think the same can be said of single adults in parishes. The Church is not holy because singles are welcome, but because they belong.

#9 *Sex: Everyone Is Doing It*—There is a stereotype that being single equals sleeping around, and if you're not willing to sleep with someone, then you must be coldhearted or asexual. Attached to this myth is the perception that everyone has sex on the third date (not true), and that having sex is the only way to satisfy your need for intimacy (also not true). In regard to being single, my sister once asked me, "Are you sure you're not a lesbian?" Had she forgotten about all the guys I dated in high school and college? What bothered me more than anything else was that I needed some valid excuse for why I wasn't dating anyone. Even my sarcastic standby, "But Jesus was single..." didn't quite fly with her.

Widowed, Divorced, and Separated Single Life

Although Beth's challenge to the many myths about being single came from her experience as a person who has never married, her insights are also valid for the lives of those formerly married. Not all single people are single by choice. Divorce or the death of a spouse forces some people into single life. Such occurrences are normally accompanied by grieving and a sense of loss. Often there is anger, depression, and maybe even despair. Knobbe's insights deserve reflection:

- "Singleness is an invitation to discover who we are."
- "Life does not start only the moment you walk down the aisle."
- "We can each be a complete person on our own."
- "Perhaps God has some greater purpose in mind for my single years."
- "My life isn't broken. Being single is not a problem that needs to be fixed."
- "In true solitude we open ourselves to God's presence here and now."
- "As single people we need friends, men and women, to challenge, guide, advise, and help us."

It is helpful to recognize that to come to acceptance and make peace with an involuntary single life, we must forgive. Even when single life comes because of the death of a spouse, it is often necessary for the survivor to "forgive" his or her partner for dying. Such feelings are not logical, but they are real. It hurts to be abandoned by someone we love. Our normal defense mechanism is to blame someone for the pain, and the easiest person to blame is the deceased. Of course, God often gets a large share of the blame and anger too.

The grieving process normally includes coming to forgiveness. This is especially true in cases of divorce and separation. Many a marriage has come to an end when one of the spouses simply decides, "It's over. I don't love you anymore. I don't want to be married—at least not to you. I'm outta here!" It's especially devastating if the one leaving has already entered into a relationship with a new partner.

Often in these circumstances civil divorce does not mean that either party is free to remarry in the Church. In some circumstances it may be possible for a divorced person to receive a declaration of nullity (annulment) of the marriage, and thereby be free to marry. But in many cases the Church cannot grant such a declaration because it cannot be shown that the marriage was invalid. Divorced persons without a declaration of nullity cannot be admitted to the sacrament of matrimony. They are expected to live a "married single life."

In these circumstances the forgiveness essential for peace of mind is a process. It takes time and repeated effort. Such a single life might seem a burden, an instance of the cross which the disciple of Christ must shoulder and carry after him.

Singles in the Christian Tradition

If single people are something of an anomaly in our contemporary culture (matchmaking sites and singles clubs are usually geared toward getting their clientele married), tradition suggests that the single life was a welcome part of the Christian culture from its first appearance. Jesus was single. Apparently Martha, Mary, and Lazarus were too.

Paul wrote to the Corinthians about marriage and sexual relations, but added, "I wish everyone to be as I am [celibate], but each has a particular gift from God" (see 1 Corinthians 7:7). Frédéric Ozanam, founder of the St. Vincent de Paul Society, never married, nor did the founder of the Catholic Worker movement, Dorothy Day. Their single state freed them up for service.

The Church urges those who are single to accept responsibility for bringing the Gospel into the world around them. All the Christian faithful share in that endeavor, but single people may find that they have unique opportunities to give witness to Christ, especially in living a chaste and celibate life. Some singles find that partnering with others of a like mind as members of third orders, oblates, or associates provides opportunities for promoting their spiritual lives and helping those in need.

We have to admit that of all four vocations, the single life receives the least attention from theologians, spiritual writers, and the hierarchy. The celibate state of the religious life and Holy Orders seems to make theological sense. The celibacy of the single life may be more difficult to evaluate, but it is not for that reason any less a witness to the values of God's kingdom. Documents written in the early centuries of the Church reveal a great respect for virginity and refer favorably to men and women who live their lives without entering into marriage.

Questions for Reflection

1. What is your view of the single life? Do you see it as a valid alternative to married life?

2. Can "forced" single life ever become a healthy way of living?

3. What can the Church do to support those in the single life?

CHAPTER THREE

Marriage

The Church's teaching on marriage begins with the conviction that the married state was established by the Creator, and its benefits and purpose are protected by divine law. The purpose of marriage is twofold: the good of the spouses (the unitive purpose) and the good of children (the procreative purpose).

The bishops at the Second Vatican Council highlighted the procreative purpose, noting that, "by its nature the institution of marriage and married love is ordered to the procreation and education of children" (*Gaudium et Spes*, 48). This sacred trust (sharing in God's creative power and caring for the children born of their mutual expression of married love) demands total fidelity and an unbreakable bond. The unitive purpose, then, is vital to married life. Married love springs from divine love and ought to be modeled on Christ's love for his spouse, the Church.

Preparing for Marriage

Deacon William Urbine, a licensed marriage and family therapist, offers suggestions for couples preparing for marriage. He advises couples to assess whether they have the obvious and essential tool for their journey together, namely, good communication. Ask any married couple—they'll tell you how making a real effort to talk about and work through everyday concerns is crucial to their stability and sanity. It also builds the trust, courage, and skills that ground the spirit of love.

Being able to talk over everything with your spouse (or future spouse) makes for a vital relationship. It doesn't matter whether the subject matter is how a family member really upsets you or even if it is about an annoying mannerism of your fiancé(e). By talking it out and listening regularly, patiently, you develop the skills and trust to tackle any major issues that may arise.

The deacon's second piece of advice is related to the first: Learn how to fight fair. As a couple, do you resolve issues well? Most married couples have a few standard ongoing fights. They might include children, sex (or the lack of it), finances, in-laws, and hurt feelings. Every couple's list might be slightly different, yet there are some similarities as well.

Perhaps you have already figured out what five fights you will have over the lifetime of a marriage. Jot them down. Now, try to figure out what you can do differently with your responses to make your arguments more constructive. Figuring out the best time of day to talk is very helpful. If a heated conflict should happen during the day, it is also important that you have agreed in principle (*and* in practice) not to go to bed before resolving the concern.

Third on Urbine's list is to be prepared to accept change. Openness to trying out new things is important. This can range from going out to a new restaurant to switching parenting roles. You've already changed some because of this new relationship. Sometimes changes are beyond our control. We don't ask for them. Perhaps it is a job loss with a required relocation to a new town or maybe it is a child with a disability demanding your undivided attention. We might also be overwhelmed by our work, a new career, or the changes in roles in our relationships. Whatever these changes are, coping with them well is important. Seeking feedback from family and friends on how you're handling change can help.

Learning to accept your in-laws is also important. They are the people who have shaped and formed the one with whom you will spend your life. Do you like your future in-laws? Can you imagine loving them? How do they compare with your own family? Whether they are quiet or loud, touchy-feely with lots of hugs and kisses, or more aloof, your future spouse has been strongly shaped by his or her family.

Sometimes your future spouse will have personality traits very similar to those you have observed in his or her family members. Can you live with these qualities or traits or do they upset you? When we are deeply in love we may overlook how strong the past influences of family will be in our relationship. Patience and understanding, as well as honesty, are important.

Another essential area of concern for couples preparing for marriage is children. You should have some conversations about the number of children you want and when you want to start your family. Do you want a large or small family? How do you want to parent these children? If you haven't had these conversations, start talking. What qualities in your future spouse might you want to see in your own children?

Children are an exciting part of a marriage, but they are demanding and draining. You need to decide early, ideally before marriage, how your children will be raised in your religious faith, especially if your partner is of another faith tradition. Perhaps one or both of you bring children to the marriage. How are they adjusting to their future stepparent, and how is your future spouse adjusting to them? One hopes there is a comfort level with them and a genuine acceptance on your future spouse's part. It's also consoling to see grandparents on both sides accepting these children.

Intimacy in marriage is an essential component of happy married life. Being intimate—now that can be lots of fun, you say. It's fun to laugh and play together and enjoy each other's company. It's great to be romantic. But there's much more to intimacy than sleeping together. Sharing feelings, conflicts, crisis, faith, the beauty of nature, working together, sex and romance, talking about ideas that matter to us, the many ways we have fun together—these all are a part of being married. Each of them provides a path toward intimacy.

Caution: Some couples use sex to resolve conflicts, to bypass the *work* of developing friendship. Sexual intimacy can be a wonderful form of communication, but it also can leave problems unresolved.

Last but not least on Urbine's list is openness to God. Openness to God's working in our lives makes all the difference. Acknowledging and sharing that God is in the middle of your lives, guiding you in the big and small changes, makes a marriage. Feeling God's presence in your daily lives can be very reassuring. On the other hand, sometimes it is hard to accept that God's ways are not always our ways. In either case, God's grace is a key ingredient in your finding happiness together.

Couples need to find ways to share faith and beliefs with each other, whether or not they follow all the same rituals. Expression of your faith will bind you to each other as disciples journeying together along the way. These expressions can be as simple as praying together before meals or taking time to stand in wonder before God's creation on a walk or on vacation. They can be routine involvement in the worship and activities of your local parish.

Keys to Understanding Marriage

In 2010 the United States Catholic bishops wrote "Marriage: Love and Life in the Divine Plan"—a letter to promote and defend marriage. John Feister outlined seven aspects in the bishops' letter that may be helpful for married couples to assess:

1. **Marriage is a sign of the relationship between Christ and the Church.** From early on in the Church's history Christians recognized that the relationship between husbands and wives is sacred. Church Father St. Clement of Alexandria wrote around AD 205, "The truly happy marriage must be judged by neither wealth nor beauty but by virtue."

2. **Marriage has two purposes: unitive and procreative.** In plain talk, married couples love one another and, when the gift is given, raise children. These two purposes of marriage are intimately related. The Second Vatican Council described marriage as a partnership of life and love. Properly committed to at the outset, it is a lifelong bond that couples must remain committed to, a "faithful, privileged sphere of intimacy between spouses that lasts until death."

That intimacy is expressed, of course, in "conjugal love," the sexual intimacy shared between woman and man in marriage, a "complete and total gift" of one to the other. Sexual intimacy is a key part, leading to, in the words of Vatican II's *Gaudium et Spes*, "free and mutual self-giving, experienced in tenderness and action, and permeating their entire lives; this love is developed and increased by its generous exercise."

3. **Marriage helps everybody.** The bishops point out that marriage is not a private institution: It is the foundation of the family and is essential for all of society. They decry a growing trend that sees marriage as something of a private matter, separate from child-rearing, "an individualistic project not related to the common good but oriented mostly to achieving personal satisfaction.... Thus the decision to marry is seen as one thing; the decision to bear children another. When children are viewed in this way, there can be damaging consequences not only for them but also for the marriage itself."

4. **Marriage is a sacrament.** The sacramental nature of marriage was explained most clearly at the Second Vatican Council, in which the bishops quote: "Spouses, therefore, are fortified and, as it were, consecrated for the duties and dignity of their state by [this] special sacrament; fulfilling their conjugal and family role by virtue of this sacrament, spouses are penetrated with the spirit of Christ and their whole life is suffused by faith, hope and charity; thus they increasingly further their own perfection and their mutual sanctification, and together they render glory to God" (*Gaudium et Spes*, 48).

5. **Marriage is mutual, healing, giving.** The married relationship is fueled by the grace of the Holy Spirit. With the help of God, then, the "spouses become willing to do the acts and courtesies of love toward each other, regardless of the feelings of the moment." Those acts and courtesies are nurtured by the self-giving life of Christ for his Church; this spills over into the spouses' relationship, into their families, into the broader Church. The bishops insist that no sacrament is given for its own sake; marriage is a sacrament, "directed toward the salvation of others" (*CCC*, #1534).

Marriage, in imitation of Christ, is a healing relationship. The love of Christ for his Church calls for a "healing relationship between man and woman." That in no way allows for one-sided subjection of wife to husband; rather, there should be a "mutual subjection of husband and wife."

6. **Our families are holy families.** Christian families are *sacramental*. Needless to say, our imperfect families can merely point to the perfect, loving relationship of our Triune God. But we families do exactly that in the ways that we love and care for one another. We are given a model to follow in the full humanity of Jesus, who was born into a human family and lived the same joys and hopes, the same struggles and difficulties, as our own families.

Let's reflect on that for a moment, as the bishops suggest. Were there disagreements in the Holy Family? How else could

Jesus be like one of us, in all ways but sin? Did Jesus learn how to make a living in his father's trade, like other young men of his day? How else could he be one of us? Mothers and fathers nurture the faith of their children in various ways, including prayer and education, teaching the virtues of love, the value of repentance and forgiveness. Christian families are called to be just that: Christian families, in spite of our culture's strong pull in other directions.

7. **Marriages are virtuous.** The dynamics of family holiness depend upon the life of grace and love nurtured in a couple's marriage. The bishops acknowledge that the yes proclaimed before the community, at the wedding, begins the real work of marriage, namely, to become an "image of Christ's love for his Church." The wedding is filled with the hope to "become what you are" as our bishops say, but they observe what long-married couples know well: "This will require persistent effort."

Romance will not always be present: A living love knows this. The bishops note what they likely have learned from experienced couples: "Getting married does not, therefore, magically confer perfection. Rather, the love to which the spouses have been configured [through the marriage sacrament] is powerful enough to transform their whole life's journey so that it becomes a journey towards perfection." All of this makes marriage a sign of the kingdom, say the bishops. Ultimately, "Christian married love is a preparation for eternal life," one that includes the entire Church.

Threats to Marriage

In his summary of the U.S. bishops' letter on marriage, Feister found four issues which the bishops consider threats to marriage in our society. These "hot-button issues" include:

- Contraception (which the bishops describe as objectively wrong)
- Same-sex unions (an attempt to redefine the nature of marriage and family, which harms the intrinsic dignity of every human person and the common good)
- Divorce (God's plan for marriage persists, and struggling couples are urged to turn to the Lord for help; no one, however, is obliged to stay in an abusive relationship)
- Cohabitation outside marriage (this violates the purpose of marriage)

Married couples are an important witness to faith and fidelity that provides a powerful counterpoint to a society which increasingly favors short-term solutions and quick fixes. If marriage is your vocation, make sure you are prepared to make a commitment that will last a lifetime.

Questions for Reflection

1. How are the unitive and procreative purposes of marriage intimately connected?

2. Which of Urbine's tools for marriage do you consider most important?

3. Which insights in the U.S. bishops' letter do you find most helpful?

CHAPTER FOUR

Holy Orders

A discussion of Holy Orders must begin with the recognition that all the baptized share in the royal priesthood of Jesus Christ. This teaching of the Church was reiterated at the Second Vatican Council: "Though they differ essentially and not only in degree, the common priesthood of the faithful and the ministerial or hierarchical priesthood are nevertheless interrelated. Each in its own particular way shares in the one priesthood of Jesus Christ" (*Lumen Gentium*, 10).

It is this common priesthood of the faithful that empowers the baptized to join in offering the Eucharist at Mass. They further exercise their priesthood by receiving the sacraments, by offering prayers, by giving witness through holy lives, and by acts of self-denial and charity.

The ministerial or hierarchical priesthood (the priesthood of Holy Orders) specially commissions a baptized person, through the gift of sacred powers, to form and govern Christ's priestly people. Acting in the person of Christ, the priest of Orders brings about the Eucharist and offers this sacrifice to God in the name of the people.

The Three Orders of Holy Orders

Holy Orders, however, includes not only the priesthood and episcopacy, but also the diaconate. The Church maintains that Jesus himself instituted the Church and gave her the authority, mission, and orientation for ministry. Through these three orders or governing bodies, the Church exercises the authority she received from Christ. By means of a religious and liturgical act, the Church ordains or consecrates a man to exercise a sacred power that comes only from Christ himself. This power has been passed on from Christ to the apostles and to their successors. The visible sign of this ordination is the laying on of hands by a bishop along with a consecratory prayer.

The first order, at a lower level of the hierarchy, is the diaconate. The bishop imposes hands on the candidate not for priesthood but for ministry. A deacon is ordained to serve, assisting priests and bishops in celebrating liturgies, and to witness marriages, proclaim the Gospel, preach, preside at funerals, and pursue various forms of charity.

The second order is the presbyterate. The Greek word *presbyteros* means "elder." The presbyter (we commonly refer to him as "priest" in light of his priestly function) is authorized to act in the person of Christ as the head of the Church. He, too, is ordained for service. His first duty is to be a prophet, "to announce the Gospel of God to all" (*Presbyterorum Ordinis*, 4). As priest the elder presides at the Eucharist as well as at other sacraments. As elder he is charged to lead the faithful and build up the Body of Christ.

The third order is the episcopacy. The Greek word *episcopos* means "supervisor." We usually refer to someone serving in this capacity as "bishop." His responsibility as a successor of the apostles is to teach, sanctify, and sustain the faithful. The bishop of Rome, also called the Roman pontiff or pope, is the bishop who is the successor of St. Peter. He holds primacy of power over all the churches.

The Diaconate

James Alt describes a deacon as a man who is called to service. Like priests and bishops, he receives the sacrament of Holy Orders. He is an ordained person living in the lifestyle of the laity. His service is threefold: service of the Word, service of the altar, and service of charity.

The role of the deacon is to be a helper of bishops and priests in service to the people of God, proclaiming by his very life the Church's call to serve the needs of others.

Well over 90 percent of deacons are married. Thus, the typical deacon attempts to balance three priorities in his life: the duties of husband and father, the responsibilities of his job or profession, and his ministry as an ordained minister.

The diaconate is as old as the Church. Acts 6:2–5 may be the first mention of deacons in the Church. As the centuries passed, however, the role of deacon became less prominent. By the end of the first millennium the decline was evident. For the next several centuries the permanent diaconate was really a non-existent ministry. The Council of Trent in the sixteenth century discussed the possibility of restoring it but nothing happened. When the idea resurfaced at the Second Vatican Council, Pope Paul VI in 1967 restored the diaconate as a permanent ministry in the Latin Rite.

The U.S. bishops' Committee on the Permanent Diaconate describes the role of the deacon in these terms:

> Deacons are not the only Christians involved in caring for the needy. But particularly and officially committed to service, the deacon is to inspire, promote and help coordinate the service that the whole Church must undertake in imitation of Christ. He has a special responsibility to identify to the Church those who are in need and particularly those who are without power or at the margins in our society. He thus becomes a

representative figure in whom the Church reaches out
to the needy and the needy challenge the Church.

Many of the liturgical functions of the deacon were spelled out
in Pope Paul VI's Apostolic Letter *Ecclesiae Sanctae II*, which
restored the diaconate. These include baptizing, bringing
viaticum to the dying, witnessing marriages, officiating at
funerals, proclaiming the Gospel at Mass both by reading and
preaching, and serving as pastoral administrator or guide for the
community when no priest is present.

Although requirements vary from diocese to diocese, among
the major criteria for acceptance into the diaconate program are:
(1) maturity; (2) active faith life; (3) stable marriage of a "reason-
able length" (if married), and spousal support; (4) physical and
emotional health; and (5) commitment to all aspects of diaconal
service.

The Presbyterate

From his decades of experience, Franciscan Fr. Thomas
Richstatter addresses the sacrament of Holy Orders and its place
in today's world. When he asks, "Is it harder to be a priest today
than it used to be?" he recalls that a parishioner wondering why
there are fewer priests these days asked him that question
recently. He said he didn't know if being a priest is *harder* than
it used to be, but it is certainly *different*.

To understand what is happening to the sacrament of Holy Orders today he suggests that we first look at the changes we Catholics have experienced in the other sacraments—especially the sacraments of baptism, Eucharist, and reconciliation.

A Catholic can hardly be unaware of the changes that have taken place in the sacrament of baptism during the past thirty years. We see catechumens being dismissed after the homily. Infants are being baptized during Sunday Eucharist. Baptismal pools are replacing holy water fonts. These external ritual and architectural changes are an indication of a deeper, internal change—a change in our understanding of the role and meaning of baptism. Since Vatican II, we have come to a new appreciation of the power and the effects of baptism. No one can be baptized and not have a role to play in the Church. Baptism and discipleship go together.

The disciples of Christ—today as in biblical times—are entrusted with carrying on the mission and ministry of Christ. As the community came to see Christ as the priest of the New Covenant, it also came to understand that every baptized Christian shares in that ministry also. The *Catechism of the Catholic Church* reminds us that the "whole community of believers is, as such, priestly" (*CCC,* #1546). We call this priesthood which is shared by all the baptized "the common priesthood of all the faithful" (*CCC,* #1547); the priesthood resulting from the sacrament of Holy Orders is called the "ministerial priesthood."

That we are all priests is not a new idea—it is as old as the Scriptures: "[L]et yourselves be built into a spiritual house, to be a holy priesthood, to offer spiritual sacrifices acceptable to God through Jesus Christ" (1 Peter 2:5). But if our common priesthood is not new, the importance given to it certainly is. This new emphasis given to baptism and the common priesthood of all the faithful has caused a flowering of ministries in the Church. In parishes around the world we now see Christians serving as readers, Communion ministers, spiritual directors, catechists, liturgists, ministers to the sick, directors of religious education, parish managers.

We are all aware of the changes that have taken place in the Mass since Vatican II. These changes have affected the role of the ordained priest. Today when Catholics talk about the role of the priest at Mass they are referring to more than the consecration: They are usually discussing the way he preaches and presides. Eucharist is a complex ritual action at which we gather to hear the Word of God proclaimed in Scripture, prayers, and homily. The priest's role is vital in all these actions.

The sacrament of Holy Orders enables the priest to speak in the name of the whole community. Just as your hand can write a signature and it binds your whole body, or your mouth can give "your word" which binds your whole person, the priest can speak in the name of the whole Body. He is ordained to say prayers to which we can all respond "Amen." Because of Holy Orders the priest "possesses the authority to act in the power and place of the person of Christ himself" (*CCC*, #1548).

Fr. Tom Richstatter recalls, "When I was ordained, the identity of the priest was closely associated with confession. The priest was the one who had the power to say with the voice of Christ, 'I absolve you from your sins.' During those first years as an ordained priest I spent more time in the course of a week hearing confessions than I did saying Mass.

"Each Saturday long lines of penitents approached the confessional. Today, in most parishes, those lines have disappeared. And yet reconciliation—striving for communion with God and one another—is the primary ministry of the Church; it is not merely something the priest does for a few minutes on Saturday afternoon." His reflections continue in the following section.

* * *

If we are to be a sacrament—a visible sign—of reconciliation, we must actively pursue those works of justice and mercy that will make this reconciliation possible. The parish must see the priest himself as a reconciling person. Otherwise, parishioners will not see him as an icon of the forgiving Christ in the sacrament of reconciliation.

It should not be surprising if the changes we have experienced in the sacraments of baptism, Eucharist, and reconciliation have brought about major changes in our understanding of the sacrament of Holy Orders. Today, the question "What is a priest?" is not an easy question to answer.

Originally "episcopate, presbyterate, and diaconate" referred to secular offices in Greek society. We cannot find any distinct job description for these three offices in early Christian writings; it seems that their function varied from place to place. Early Christians used the terms somewhat interchangeably.

But as often happened in the history of the Church, time and pastoral experience have drawn uniformity from original diversity. By the third or fourth century the variety of ministries mentioned in the New Testament was assumed into the ministry of leadership. The *episcopos*, or bishop, became the primary minister.

The bishop exercised his ministry with the help of a council of elders (presbyters) who were his coworkers. Their principal function was to advise the bishop. They shared this responsibility for the local Church and sometimes stood in for him when he was absent. The bishop also had the help of deacons who were responsible for specific ministries, for example, assistance to widows and orphans, care of the sick, finances, education, and administration. This threefold ministry continues today.

As the Christian community grew and became distinct from

Judaism, it defended and explained its rituals in contemporary terms of the day. Christians gathered for the "Breaking of the Bread" and saw this sacred meal to be the sacrament of Christ's sacrifice on Calvary. Those who presided at this sacrifice— bishops and especially presbyters—came to be called "priests." Their function began to be seen as similar to the Jewish levitical priesthood.

By the end of the third century the community leader was seen as a sacred person, one set apart to offer sacrifice on behalf of the faithful. The orders of bishops, presbyters, and deacons became sacred orders.

When I was ordained in 1966, a priest was defined as someone set apart from other Catholics. Priests wear special clothing (clerical black); we live in a special house (a rectory); we have a special lifestyle (celibacy). Today most Catholics I encounter are not especially concerned about these things. They want their priest to be one of them, someone living in the midst of their world—not someone set apart. They expect the priest to know their joys and their sorrows, their trials and their pain. The priest is expected to know how difficult it is to raise children and what it is to fear losing a job or to face an addiction.

Speaking personally, I have found that parishioners want me to know how hard they work for their money. They expect me to preach about these things so that I can bring the Gospel to their everyday experience. They want a priest who can pray with their voice, the voice of the Church. Vatican II, in its decree on the life of priests, tells me that "priests have been placed in the midst of the laity so that they may lead them all to the unity of charity..." (Decree on the Ministry and Life of Priests, 9).

I find that it is not always easy to be both set apart *and* in the midst. Parishioners expect me, as a priest, to be engaged in this world. As parishioners see me up close it becomes more evident to them that sometimes my words come from Christ and other times they come from my own ignorance, prejudice, and even sometimes from my sinfulness. Reconciliation between people of different social and economic classes, races, religions, and political parties is a difficult if not impossible task. Yet I am instructed by the Second Vatican Council that the priest has the task of "bringing about agreement among divergent outlooks in such a way that nobody may feel a stranger in the Christian community" (Decree on the Ministry and Life of Priests, 9).

Ministry becomes the place in which the priest encounters the Holy Spirit. I am a better preacher when I know the congregation's hopes and fears, joys and sorrows. Living in the midst of the parish—visiting homes, attending wedding receptions, helping build a house—these are not distractions from prayer but are the source of my prayer. The parish is the sacrament, the window, through which the priest views God.

The tension between being set apart and living in the midst is perhaps a reflection of the tension between the sacraments of

Holy Orders and baptism. As the Church passes from century to century, each age discovers a way to synthesize this tension.

St. Augustine spoke of it in this way during the fourth century: "The day I became a bishop, a burden was laid on my shoulders.... Indeed, it terrifies me to think that I could take more pleasure in the honor attached to my office, which is where its danger lies, than in your salvation, which ought to be its fruit. This is why being set above you fills me with alarm, whereas being with you gives me comfort. Danger lies in the first; salvation in the second" (*Liturgy of the Hours*, reading for September 19).

In these difficult times we might do well to learn from St. Augustine. He spoke of the dangers inherent in being set above others and the salvation that comes from our common baptism. Today, we do well to understand the sacrament of Holy Orders and the ordained priesthood within the context of the priest-hood that we all share in virtue of our baptism.

Priesthood in Crisis

Fr. James Martin assesses the decline in the number of priests. He believes that the decline in ordained priestly vocations can be attributed to several causes.

The Second Vatican Council reminded people that it's not simply priests who have a vocation—everyone has a baptismal call. Catholics today see more than one way to follow the discipleship of Jesus. This may have led to less of a desire for the priesthood and religious life.

The second cause may be the decline in religiosity in Western culture. That naturally affects priestly vocations. The third cause may be a lack of desire for long-term commitment. Divorce rates have risen, couples marry later, and it's harder for young people to make lifelong commitments.

Finally, there is a decline in the respect given to celibacy, which today is seen more as a negative than as a positive—that is, a way of loving many people freely and deeply.

The priest, in recent decades, is also no longer seen as the *only* mediator between the people and God. Happily, the faithful appreciate more their own participatory role in Mass. Prior to Vatican II, the priest and altar, for example, faced the same way the people faced as a sign of deep reverence to God. The turning around of the altar—which expressed that reverence in a new way by reminding us of the presence of God in the faithful—was an important symbol for the Second Vatican Council.

Some years ago, Bishop Kenneth Untener, of Saginaw, Michigan, when speaking to a group of soon-to-be-ordained Jesuits, mentioned that he liked to play the piano. Then he sat down at a piano and said, "I'd like to play you a song." The bishop sang (on his own) a familiar hymn. Then he said, "Now I'd like you to sing along with me." We obliged by singing along. Then he said, "What did you think of the first version?"

Wondering where this was all going, we said, "Well, it was enjoyable listening to you!"

He continued, "And what did you think about the *second* version?" And we said, "Well, it was fun to participate with you and to sing along."

Then the bishop said with a smile, "The first version is the priesthood *before* Vatican II; the second version is the priesthood *after* Vatican II." It was a good illustration of what happened after Vatican II: The faithful became more involved in not just the Mass but also the Church; they have a greater role; they participate more with the priest. They were certainly participating before, but now it's more overt. The same is true in our broader understanding of vocation and the "universal call to holiness" (see *Lumen Gentium*, 5).

One of the frequently proposed solutions to the priestly vocation crisis is the ordination of married men, a practice of the first thousand years in the history of the Church. Recall that St. Peter was a married man. There are those who oppose our having a married clergy, arguing that priestly celibacy is a thousand-year-old tradition that, many believe, has been guided by the Holy Spirit. Of course an interesting recent development in that custom is acceptance of married Episcopalian priests into the Roman rite. Also debates about ordaining women to the priesthood have been ruled out by Pope John Paul II.

One thing, however, is certain: If priestly vocations continue to fall, we will become a less Eucharistic Church. Without people to celebrate the divine worship, how can we continue to be a Church that is centered on the Eucharist?

The Episcopacy

A bishop is a priest who has been ordained to be a successor to the apostles, a member of the episcopal body that is the successor to the college of apostles in their role as teachers and pastors. In the words of Vatican II, "Together with their head, the Supreme Pontiff, and never apart from him, they have supreme and full authority over the universal Church" (*Lumen Gentium*, 22).

Questions for Reflection

1. Do you think most Catholics think of themselves in terms of the common priesthood of the faithful?
2. Has restoration of the permanent diaconate helped the Church in our modern era?
3. Is the role of the priest understood and respected today?

CHAPTER FIVE

Religious Life

The common denominator for those in religious life (whether they are sisters, brothers, or religious priests) is the vow to practice the so-called evangelical counsels, which are chastity, poverty, and obedience. These counsels are drawn from the New Testament. Jesus suggests that some of his followers will renounce marriage "for the sake of the kingdom of heaven," (see Matthew 19:11–12), hence the vow of chastity. He then warns how difficult it is for the rich to enter the kingdom of heaven (see Matthew 19:23), hence the vow of poverty. And the vow of obedience is the self-denial he requires of his disciples living in complete subjection to a religious superior (see Matthew 16:24).

The Evangelical Counsels

Chastity is the traditional name for the vow to observe permanent sexual abstinence. Some writers prefer to call it virginity, arguing that even married people are called to be chaste, that is, to use their sexuality in ways appropriate to their state in life. Since one can become a religious even after having engaged in sexual behavior, virginity falters too as an adequate term. In reality the religious vows not to marry and promises to live a life of chastity in celibacy. The vow not to marry and be chaste is supposed to free the religious to focus more faithfully upon God.

Poverty, too, is a relative term. Most of those who take the vow of poverty, unlike the impoverished, have adequate food, clothing, and shelter. Their vow is a form of material asceticism, that is, a renunciation of unnecessary worldly goods. In imitation of Jesus's lifestyle, the religious agree to live frugally and to identify with the struggles of the world's poor. The vow of poverty is supposed to thwart the desire for more earthly possessions and help the religious focus on the things of heaven.

Obedience is the promise to obey the formal rule or constitution of the religious order or institute to which the religious belongs. This surrender of autonomy includes submission to the authority and direction of the legitimate leader of the community as well. Religious try to think of obedience to the commands of the community and its leadership as obedience to

Christ. The vow of obedience is supposed to counter pride and egotism and help the religious focus on doing the will of God.

History of Religious Life

The roots of religious life as a vocation go back to the earliest centuries of the Church, when a small number of Christians devoted themselves to ascetical practices (e.g., fasting, celibacy, hours in prayer, and living in isolation as hermits) as a way of giving themselves totally to Christ. The fourth-century St. Anthony of Egypt is an example. His ascetical practices and way of life attracted others to his hermitage in the desert, and soon small groups or cells of disciples and masters sprang up in imitation.

When Constantine legalized the Christian religion in AD 312 and widespread persecution and martyrdom ended, some Christians looked for ways of dying for Christ by living intensely the values of the Gospel. St. Pachomius is usually credited with establishing monastic compounds and writing a rule for the monks to follow. St. Jerome, St. Augustine, and St. Benedict continued to develop communities, practices, and rules for religious in the consecrated life. St. Francis of Assisi and St. Dominic contributed further to the formation of religious communities and urged their followers to be actively involved in spreading the Gospel and meeting the needs of the impoverished.

As might be expected the history of religious life and religious communities is marked with times of growth and times of decline. There is a joke that suggests that even God doesn't know how many religious institutes there really are. We do know that there are more than 70,000 sisters, 5,000 brothers, and 14,000 religious priests across the United States.

Following the publication of Thomas Merton's autobiography *The Seven Storey Mountain* in 1948 there was a dramatic increase in the number of applicants for the Trappist monastery, the Abbey of Gethsemani, near Bardstown, Kentucky.

Is God Calling Me?

Elizabeth Bookser Barkley confirms that the decision to be or not to be a religious is not always easy. She recalls the story of Br. Mark Ligett who, as a first-grader, stood up in the classroom and proudly announced to the Franciscan sister teaching his class that he knew what he wanted to be when he grew up: "a Franciscan nun!"

After explaining that only women could become sisters, his teacher suggested that he think about becoming a Franciscan brother. Years later, Br. Mark did just that. He joined the Franciscans and continued to pray, listen, and discern his call before making a commitment to consecrated life.

Several years into formation, he felt a strong call toward deeper prayer than an active order could afford him. So he received permission to join the Trappist monastery in Gethsemani, Kentucky, where he lived a cloistered life devoted to prayer, quiet, and community. After a year he returned to the Franciscans, took his final vows, left again a few years later to rejoin the Trappists, and then returned once more to the Franciscans.

A Trappist abbot told Br. Mark that in his struggle he was like St. Francis, always trying to balance an active life and prayer. "I know now," Br. Mark concluded, "the Franciscan life is where I belong."

Renewal of Religious Life

Even though religious life has been a part of the Church from early on, the bishops at the Second Vatican Council both applauded the men and women who have dedicated themselves to the consecrated life and encouraged the ongoing renewal of their religious communities. In 1966 Pope Paul VI issued a series of norms to help in implementing the Second Vatican Council's call for renewal. He urged that the following be normative for all religious orders and their members:

- The Divine Office (the Church's official set of prayers for various hours during the day) should be prayed in full or in part on a daily basis
- Mental prayer (contemplation) should be pursued more vigorously

- Religious should not neglect acts of penance and mortification
- Assessment and promotion of the spirit and practice of poverty
- Community life should be a priority, including time for recreation

In 1969 the Vatican's Sacred Congregation of Religious and Secular Institutes provided additional guidelines and principles for ongoing renewal. Again in 1971 the same Sacred Congregation issued further encouragement for renewal, recognizing the differing needs of the various orders based on whether they were dedicated to contemplative life (communities dedicated solely to prayer), or to apostolic life (active communities dedicated to spreading the Gospel), or to a combination of contemplation and the active apostolate.

The Spirit of the Religious Life

All religious orders were encouraged to review the spirit and intention of their respective founders. The Sisters and Daughters of Charity, for example, were to reassess their charism and the purpose for which Elizabeth Ann Seton founded their community. The Franciscans were to recall the spirit and intention of Francis of Assisi. The Benedictines were to judge their rule and practice in the light of their founder, Benedict.

Prayer, silence, the Eucharist, liturgy, the needs of the world, and a sense of sharing in the Church's mission are essential elements in religious renewal and spiritual growth. All religious men and women, whether hidden behind monastery walls or actively engaged in public ministry, are to be living witnesses of God's love. And one of the chief characteristics of each community is supposed to be simplicity, reflective of the true disciple's dependence upon God.

Luke records in chapter six of his Gospel the advice of Jesus: Don't worry about your life, about what you will eat or wear. God knows what you need. Let your priority be the kingdom. Sell your belongings, give alms. Have no fear. Your heavenly Father will give you the kingdom.

In effect the religious person undertakes a different lifestyle in order to make a difference. Each religious sister, brother, priest, or monk is trying to cause a revolution by self-transformation. To many people their effort seems impotent if not foolish, but in the economy and culture of the kingdom of God one lone righteous person makes a majority.

Most dioceses have vocation offices. A number of religious orders have sites online. The information provided by these services can be helpful in discerning whether one has a religious vocation and which of the religious orders is the appropriate one for living out that commitment. Those who are uncertain about making a lifelong commitment may be interested in joining third order or associate programs which are open to laypeople who wish to support the mission of a religious order.

Some men in religious life choose to become priests. Normally they live out this dual vocation in a particular community, such as in the Society of Jesus (Jesuits) or the Franciscans.

Questions for Reflection

1. How do the evangelical counsels help one become more dedicated to Christ and the Gospel?
2. What makes a religious vocation attractive?
3. Have you known any religious sisters or brothers whose dedication you admire?

Sources

Alt, James L. "Deacons Today: Ministers of Service." *Catholic Update,* June 1997.

Barkley, Elizabeth Bookser. "Father, Sister, Brother, Deacon: Is God Calling Me?" *Catholic Update,* October 2010.

Feister, John. "Seven Keys to Marriage: A Married Person Looks at the Bishops' New Pastoral *Marriage: Love and Life in the Divine Plan.*" *Catholic Update,* June 2010.

Knobbe, Beth M. *Party of One: Living Single With Faith, Purpose, and Passion* (Cincinnati: St. Anthony Messenger Press, 2011).

Martin, James, S.J. "The Priesthood Today: We're All in This Together." *Catholic Update,* July 2009.

Richstatter, Thomas, O.F.M. "Sacrament of Holy Orders: Priesthood in Transition." *Catholic Update,* July 1997.

Thibodeaux, Mark E., S.J. "Praydreaming: Key to Discernment." *Catholic Update,* February 2010.

Tracy, Fidelis, C.D.P. "Vocations: How Is God Calling Me?" *Catholic Update,* August 2001.

Urbine, William. "Preparing for Marriage: 10 Tools for the Journey." *Catholic Update,* June 2006.

USCCB. *United States Catholic Catechism for Adults* (Washington, D.C.: USCCB, 2006).

Contributors

James L. Alt is a freelance writer and consulting editor for *Deacon Digest*.

Elizabeth Bookser Barkley is a freelance writer and professor of English at Mt. St. Joseph College, Cincinnati, Ohio.

John Feister is editor-in-chief of *St. Anthony Messenger* magazine. He has master's degrees in humanities and theology from Xavier University in Cincinnati, Ohio.

Beth M. Knobbe is a campus minister at the Sheil Catholic Center of Northwestern University, popular speaker on young adult spirituality, and author of *Party of One: Living Single With Faith, Purpose, and Passion,* and *Finding My Voice: A Young Woman's Perspective.*

James Martin, S.J., is culture editor of *America* magazine, and author of *The Jesuit Guide to (Almost) Everything.*

Thomas Richstatter, O.F.M., S.T.D., teaches at St. Meinrad (Indiana) School of Theology.

Mark E. Thibodeaux, S.J., is the author of *Armchair Mystic* and *God, I Have Issues: 50 Ways to Pray No Matter How You Feel.*

Fidelis Tracy, C.D.P., is the former vocation coordinator for the Congregation of Divine Providence, Melbourne, Kentucky.